Labyrinth Prayer Stations

Ian Tarrant
Senior Anglican Chaplain, University of Nottingham

Sally Dakin
Ordinand, St Albans and Oxford Ministry Course

GROVE BOOKS LIMITED
RIDLEY HALL RD CAMBRIDGE CB3 9HU

Contents

The Cover Illustration is by Peter Ashton

Acknowledgments

Many have contributed directly or indirectly to this booklet; but particular thanks are due to those who have shared their work with us, and amongst them special thanks to Patrick Angier who set Ian exploring the theme in the first place, and to Paul Breckell who was responsible for linking the two authors.

Copyright

The text of this booklet is copyright Ian Tarrant and Sally Dakin, apart from the example prayer journeys which are copyright the authors named on them. If these are used for public worship without significant modification, then acknowledgement should be made to both the author of the journey and to this booklet.

Copyright © Ian Tarrant and Sally Dakin 2004

First Impression August 2004
ISSN 0144-1728
ISBN 1 85174 568 8

What's This All About?

In recent years a number of churches have experimented with 'prayer journeys' or 'labyrinths' in which a number of 'prayer stations' are visited in sequence. There have also been a number of experiments with 'liquid worship' which are in some ways similar.

Before we go much further, it will be helpful to define some terms — recognizing that others may use the same words slightly differently, and that in the course of time popular usage may opt for different meanings. But for the present we need some handles with which to grasp the things we are talking about.

- **Prayer station** — a small place, with something to look at or do, which will stimulate meditation and prayer.
- **Prayer journey** — a number of prayer stations which are to be visited in sequence.
- **Labyrinth** — a convoluted path which is followed as an aid to meditation and prayer, perhaps with prayer stations en route.
- **Prayer fayre** — a number of prayer stations which may be visited in any order.[1]
- **Liquid worship** — a collection of prayer stations and other activities (such as singing or group Bible study) which the participants may visit in any order they please.

Having made these definitions, it is worth noting a tendency to use the word labyrinth to describe all prayer journeys, but this seems to us a devaluation of the term.

Some would want to class liquid worship and prayer journeys as examples of 'alternative worship' and we would not want to argue with that — but we are happy to allow others to define the boundaries of 'alternative worship.'[2]

The labyrinth which housed the minotaur of Greek mythology must have been a complex path with branches, for Theseus needed a ball of thread to find his way out. But the labyrinth set into the floor of Chartres cathedral has no branches, nor do most labyrinths made in modern times. Nowadays the word maze is normally used to describe a perplexing branched path.

The labyrinth of Chartres was not the first labyrinth used for Christian prayer. WH Matthews[3] and H Kern[4] identify the earliest example of a labyrinth in a Christian context—a 2.5m square ornament on a pavement of the fourth century Basilica of St Reparatus, at Orléansville, Algeria.[5] Having the words *Sancta Ecclesia* at the centre, there is no doubt that this is a Christian artefact, though one can only guess how it was used. Matthews details a number of labyrinths in European churches and cathedrals, mostly in France and Italy. Labyrinths have also been used by other faith communities around the world and through the ages.[6]

A prayer journey based on the arrest, trial and crucifixion of Jesus, known as the Stations of the Cross, also has a long history, which can be traced back to pilgrims to Jerusalem walking the route from the house of Pilate to the place of the Cross.[7]

We might note also that the flower festivals which are traditional in some Anglican churches, where the church is decorated with flowers, and each corner or window is given a theme, can also approximate to prayer journeys when the themes are suitably spiritual.

However, much of the present interest in labyrinths and prayer journeys can be traced to the labyrinth set up for a week in St Paul's Cathedral, London, in March 2000, to mark the end of the second millennium of the Christian era. The path was marked on a large sheet of hessian floor covering, there were eleven stations en route, and each participant listened through personal headphones to a recorded commentary, with music and other sound effects. This labyrinth later went on tour, being set up for periods of a few days in cathedrals and other places all over the country. Subsequently materials were made available so that anyone could reproduce this labyrinth in their own church or hall[8]. Simulations also appeared on the world-wide web[9] and on CD-ROM[10].

A typical home-grown labyrinth today might consist of six to a dozen stations following a Bible story or a biblical theme, or taking the Lord's Prayer one line at a time. Each station offers a different *idea* for prayer, and preferably a physical *activity* to make the idea and the prayer more real to the participant. A route can be marked out in various ways, such as with masking tape on the floor, or defined by carefully positioned portable screens. Normally the participants begin the journey one by one at intervals, and proceed from station to station as fast as they like. The setting might be:

- an evening meeting of a church youth group
- a Saturday when the church is set up in this way and people are encouraged to come at any time during the day to make the jour-

ney at their own pace. (A suitably welcoming notice might even entice passers-by or tourists to come and try it. Could this be a form of evangelism?)

- a Christian conference, or a school or a university, where a room is set aside for this kind of prayer over a period of some days.

We might mention at this point another recent prayer phenomenon—24/7 prayer rooms, set up by churches, at conferences and at colleges, where a number of Christians resolve to maintain an unbroken time of prayer for a whole week. A room is prepared with a number of aids for prayer, much like the prayer stations which we describe in this booklet, and individuals sign up to cover one or more periods during the week. Since 1999 these prayer weeks have been held in more than 40 countries, networked and resourced through a website www.24-7prayer.com.[11]

How do prayer journeys compare with conventional Christian worship? Normal corporate worship consists of songs, readings and prayers shared simultaneously by a congregation. However when members of a Christian community experience a prayer journey, each person encounters every element of the journey, but they do so in their own time and at their own pace.

In a church service, I might be struck by the wording or the meaning of a particular prayer—but before I am able to reflect upon it in depth, the worship leader is bidding me sing a song or listen to a reading. However, when I encounter a phrase or an image that strikes a chord during a prayer journey, I can linger at that station and savour its meaning and implications for me. Is a prayer journey then an act of personal spirituality as opposed to the corporate spirituality of a service? You might argue that it is, but one has to remember that even in a church service the various elements will be experienced differently by the diverse individuals who attend. Moreover, the prayer journey is a corporate experience in that all who have taken part will have some common memories. This corporate dimension can strengthened in a number of ways:

- prayer stations where people leave artwork or 'graffiti';
- a guest book at the end of the journey, so that people can record their reactions for others to read;
- encouraging those who have finished, or not yet begun, to sit quietly nearby and pray for those now on the journey;
- an adjacent place for refreshments, where people can discuss how the journey was for them;
- a short act of worship, perhaps just a prayer and a song, for all the participants when they have finished. Obviously this option will be dependent on the ability and willingness of participants to stay and wait for the last person to finish!

2

The Journey

Archaeological remains of labyrinths, dating from diverse eras, have been found in many different parts of the world.

The study of their differences and similarities, simply as geometric figures, has occupied many minds.[12] They appear to have no 'practical' function, so it is generally assumed that they were used for recreational or spiritual purposes. Some have linked labyrinths to fertility or to an earth-goddess, perhaps seeing the labyrinth as a representation of the womb.

The Christian church, at least in the middle ages, has made use of labyrinths, and there is some evidence that walking a labyrinth was seen as an alternative to making a pilgrimage to Jerusalem. Even today there are those who make labyrinths, using a variety of different materials and media, for ornament, for fun, or spiritual purposes.[13] Like the ancients, 21st century humanity is intrigued, diverted and inspired by these 'works of art.'

The journey through the labyrinth can have a number of different qualities which affect the mood of the walker:

- calm—you have to slow down to follow the twisting path;
- obedience—following the route and surrendering the urge to wander;
- repetition—each part of the labyrinth is much like another;
- integration—body and mind working together;
- isolation—a number of 'walls' separate the walker from the world.

Little wonder that a number of faiths have used labyrinths as spiritual tools.

Some might criticize the use of labyrinths for Christian prayer and meditation because of their pagan associations, but the same accusations might be levelled at mountaintops, forests and riverbanks which so many Christians find helpful as places of prayer. Surely a labyrinth, like a mountaintop, can be accepted as a gift from God, and made holy by what the Christian does with it? There is a fair amount of Christian writing, mostly emanating from the United States, on walking and praying stationless labyrinths.[14] The classic labyrinth journey is seen as having three phases—the journey in, the time at the centre, and the journey out. These phases may be compared with the different stages of a church service, of which the first is often seen as a time of approaching God, or 'gathering,' and the last is a sending out.

In the rest of this booklet, we want to focus on prayer journeys—paths that do have stations. Obviously, setting up Christian prayer stations on a labyrinthine path is a way of dedicating that path to God. The stations give direction to the meditation and prayers of the participants. As Christians we think of life as a journey with a beginning and a goal, with meaning and purpose. Visiting the stations in a particular order has two advantages. The participants are freed from having to choose where to go next after each station. Furthermore, the material prepared is encountered in the optimum sequence, taking the participant through a series of teaching points or spiritual milestones.

Here are some possible defining themes for prayer journeys, in which the sequence of the stations is important:

- the sweep of salvation history from creation to the new Jerusalem;
- the life of a Bible character, such as Moses, Ruth, Mary or Peter
- the story of the Exodus;
- a parable, such as the Good Samaritan or the Prodigal Son;
- the Lord's Prayer;
- the oft-quoted prayer sequence of Adoration, Confession, Thanksgiving, Supplication.

When crafting such a prayer journey, the organizers will have in mind the changes of mood and focus as the individual moves through the stations, just as one prepares a normal church service with an eye to the sequence of ideas and emotions.

So does it matter what goes on *between* the stations? Does a winding trail have some benefit, that moving from A to B in a straight line does not have? The qualities listed at the beginning of this chapter may all be seen as worthwhile. But in a restricted space, where the journey is either very short or very tortuous, following a twisting path may prove to be more a hassle than a blessing—a tedious affectation adopted for the sake of using the name 'labyrinth,' rather than a meditative interlude to aid spiritual digestion.

In practical terms, a labyrinthine path may be helpful in that the participant ahead of the walker gets more advance warning of the walker's imminent arrival. We shall come back to issues of queuing and congestion later.

We have said that the word labyrinth is generally used to describe a path without branches. But it is, of course, possible to construct a prayer journey with a choice of routes at certain points. The choice may be made at random, or in response to a question, or on the basis of age or gender. This reflects the fact that our real life paths present us with junctions—and sometimes we have the freedom to choose the high road or the low road, and sometimes the choice is not ours.[15] One of our sample labyrinths will include branches.

7

3

The Stations

When several prayer stations are arranged to form a prayer journey, they tend to lead the participant through a characteristic sequence of events.

This sequence has much in common with both formal and informal acts of worship, and usually begins with some kind of 'gathering' in order to focus attention on God. In public worship this is primarily a coming together of the people towards God; on a prayer journey it is more of a coming together of the disparate parts of ourselves towards God—an intra-personal rather than an inter-personal gathering, perhaps. In a traditional labyrinth (like Chartres), the entire journey into the centre probably served such a purpose, as the worshipper prepared to encounter God.

Here's an example of a prayer station designed to facilitate this 'journey in,' from our Advent prayer journey:

> *A basket of large pebbles and a lava lamp are placed on a low table, with a sheep-skin rug, floor cushions and low chairs around, some photos of sun and melting ice, and Bible verses such as Psalm 46.10 and Ezekiel 36.26, with this intro-duction:* 'Begin by choosing a stone. Take time to sit quietly with the stone in your hands; let the warmth of your hands slowly warm it. As you sit, know that God is present. Know his love for you; let his love warm your heart. Let his love melt the hard, cold places in your life…'

How does this prayer station work? And what is distinctive about this kind of 'active prayer'?

- **Above all, it invites active participation.** This is not an exhibit to admire, or a Station of the Cross to meditate on, but a ritual to enter into—'begin by choosing a stone…'
- **It involves a physical object and a physical act.** Both the object and the act are given meaning, in this case implied by the intro-ductory words but left fairly open for individual interpretation. This physicality, so central to active prayer, demonstrates an incarnational emphasis and a cataphatic[16] spirituality. And this focus on symbolic meaning and ritual has sacramental overtones. As with sacraments, the symbolic objects and actions can convey more

than the words; touching is as significant as looking and listening.

- **It invites a subjective response rather than an objective analysis.** 'Choosing a stone' is more an intuitive than a logical decision. Those who operate largely in cognitive mode may have trouble with this; it is sometimes helpful to suggest that they approach the whole thing as an experiment, and deliberately 'suspend judgement.'
- **It takes time.** If prayer is about two-way communication with God, it is important to allow God to speak. At the 'stones' station, participants are invited to 'take time,' to slow down, to 'Be still and know that I am God...' It takes at least five minutes to warm the stone, and the lava lamp offers a slightly mesmerizing visual focus for those who like to keep their eyes open. Background music can also help the relaxation process.

If corporate worship usually begins with some kind of 'gathering,' it usually ends with some kind of 'dismissal' as the people re-orient themselves to service in the world and go their separate ways with God's blessing. Similarly in a traditional labyrinth the journey out from the centre was about re-viewing daily life in the light of an encounter with God. This prayer station was designed to facilitate the 'journey out' at the end of an Old Year/ New Year prayer journey:

> *Several sets of up to ten footprints, cut out of card, in various colours and sizes, with this introduction:* 'Take a set of footprints and find a space to arrange them. Let them represent your journey this year — and next? Offer yourself again to the One who is Lord of your past, present and future...'

Again this is all about active participation and the use of physical symbols. This time a general meaning for the symbols was suggested, with participants being invited to develop more personal meanings and to create their own ritual. As they shared their experiences afterwards, the range of meaning and action was astonishing.

If prayer journeys tend to begin with a gathering and end with a dismissal, what other prayer activities might they involve? Or, if prayer is two-way communication with God, what else needs saying or doing, and what sort of objects and actions might facilitate this? As in liturgical worship, the main ingredients are likely to be: praise and thanksgiving; self-examination, repentance and absolution; looking at, listening to and receiving from God; self-offering; and intercession. Let us consider examples to illustrate some of these.

First, a very simple 'praise' station:

> *A large pot of bubble mixture and some 'wands':* 'Instead of burning incense as a sign of worship, you could try blowing bubbles to God...'

We wondered if the participants might find this irreverent, but they seemed to enjoy it: it is an example of a slightly playful approach to spirituality which can be very liberating. After all, Jesus said, 'Become as little children.'

And a 'thank you' station, again both simple and fun:

> *Several packets of gummed paper chain strips and some felt-tips:* 'Let's make a long paper-chain expressing our thanks and praise to God! Take some strips and write a prayer of praise or thanksgiving on each... then join them onto the end of the chain.'

This prayer activity does not depend on symbolism, which may make it more accessible for some people, and the more who participate, the better. It is encouraging to read what others have written, and the length of the resulting chain (perhaps draped over the Communion table) is a visual testimony to the goodness of God.

This 'sorry' station was extremely effective:

> *A roll of foil with some pieces torn off, lots of small aluminium drinks cans, a large black dustbin full of water, with a lid, and a towel:* 'Let the foil represent things in your life you want to be free of, things you want to leave behind and move on from. Maybe you need to know God's forgiveness? Tear off a piece of foil and let it represent the wrong you are turning from. Crumple it up as a sign of your repentance, and push it into a can. If you become aware of more wrong-doing, wrong-speaking or wrong-thinking, take some more foil...When you are ready, sink the can in the dustbin and shut the lid.'

This was the children's favourite station, probably because it was so very physical—and several adults commented on how liberated they felt as they submerged their can and watched it sink. To encourage people to trust God for forgiveness, various Bible verses were displayed, including Micah 7.18–19 and 1 John 1.8–9.

Depending on the setting, some participants may feel a bit self-conscious if they are new to this kind of prayer. This prayer tent, inspired by Psalm 61.4, was very private—and very popular:

> *A child's pop-up tent furnished with rugs, cushions and Bibles, with a 'Welcome' doormat outside:* 'God welcomes us into his presence—we can have a "private audience" with him whenever we like. He loves us to spend time with him "in secret"...'

To help people to reflect on what God was saying to them at a New Year conference for people of several nationalities, we used a large table:

> *A paper tablecloth covering the table, with Bibles in various languages and marker pens:* 'What has God been saying to you this year? What is God saying to you today? Take time to respond to him. Use this cloth to write down a Scripture (in any language) through which God has spoken to you—and with which you begin the New Year.'

It is a good idea to have plenty of Bibles about on any prayer journey, so people can look up verses which come to them. Strategically placed boxes of tissues are also useful, and a notice at the end of a prayer journey suggesting where to go for pastoral help or prayer ministry may be appropriate.

In Holy Week this station was set up on the chancel step to encourage people to offer themselves and their concerns to the Christ who was crucified for them:

> *A big basket of threads, ribbons, string, wool, cut in 10–20cm pieces:* 'What do you want to bring to God today? Thanks and praise...problems... hopes and fears...pain...a difficult decision...for sin...a heavy burden...a longing for something...guilt...bitterness...joy? Choose a thread to represent each of the things you want to offer, and take them with you to the cross.'

The next station was in front of the altar:

> *A free-standing cross about 1.5m high, made of interwoven willow twigs:* 'This is the place to offer your life and everything in it to God, as he gives himself to you. Hang or tie your threads on the cross one by one, committing the things they signify to God.'[17]

As well as the introductory words at each station, we displayed various Bible verses, such as John 6.37 and Romans 5.8, and various words to inspire worship and prayer at the cross, including the Jesus Prayer and the first verses of hymns like 'When I survey,' 'My song is love unknown,' 'Rock of ages' and 'Just as I am' Sometimes the juxtaposition of new ritual and old words can be very effective, and 'something old, something new' is generally a good principle for designing prayer stations. But it is important not to overwhelm people with words; active prayer is primarily about actions.

This next example explores the contrast between the old and the new, the movement from death to life, and the idea of hope (see John 12.24):

> *A big tub of soil, a dibber, a bowl of acorns, a watering can:* 'Looking forward to the coming of God's kingdom in the world and in your life, take an acorn to reflect on. When you are ready, plant the acorn and water it, trusting yourself and all your concerns to God and his purposes.'

The last two examples illustrate different approaches to intercession.

First, using a rosary:[18]

> *Several large 'rosaries' made of beads of various shapes, sizes, colours and textures, a bowl of smaller beads, needles, bead elastic, scissors:* 'Try using one of these big "rosaries" in prayer—let each bead represent someone you would like to pray for. If you would like to, you can make a small rosary to take away with you. You could keep it in your pocket—or wear it on your wrist!'

Most of the stations mentioned so far are rather solitary, but activities like this one can be very companionable as people work side by side and perhaps tell each other something about the people their beads represent. If the prayer journey involves sitting on chairs at the stations (rather than on the floor), this is one of the places where more than one chair could be provided.

Secondly, to inspire prayer for the local community:

> *A very large sheet of paper, local newspapers and leaflets, scissors, glue, marker pens:* 'Here you can pray for the needs of the community. Cut out anything which you would like to include in prayer, and stick it onto the big sheet of paper. Add your own words if you wish. Pray for your concerns, and for issues others have identified.'

Rather like the paper-chain described above, this can have a powerful cumulative effect as more and more people add to the 'collage' and respond to others' contributions—and the sometimes very direct prayers in childish hand-writing can be a challenge to the faith of adults.

Sometimes an art and/or craft area is provided as an adjunct to a prayer journey, as a way of enabling people to respond creatively to the whole experience. The materials do not need to be sophisticated, perhaps just crayons, paints and paper, and perhaps some basic resources for collage. People might like to take their work with them (like the rosaries above) or leave them as an expression of their experience for others to see.

Although prayer stations are often arranged in a particular order as a prayer journey, perhaps with a particular theme, it is sometimes better to provide a collection of stations which can be visited in any order. There can still be a theme—perhaps very general, like Pentecost, or Psalm 23, or water—but no liturgical sequence, and people can visit as many or as few of the stations as they like. This works well if a lot of people are to experience the prayer fayre in a short time, perhaps before or after a corporate act of worship—or if the idea of 'active prayer' is very new. It can also work wonderfully in a café/bar context, where there is a prayer area as well as an eating/drinking/socializing area, and perhaps live music too.

How Can We Try This? 4

Perhaps you are keen to put some of these ideas into practice.

Before you go and buy mats, mirrors and masking tape, do some thinking and some praying and some planning. In particular, consider:

The Participants

Who is this prayer journey going to be for—the whole church community? A wider group? Or a smaller group? What time and place will suit these people best? What assumptions and experiences unite them—and what differences in ability or knowledge do you need to be aware of? What about people with disabilities? (This kind of prayer can be especially helpful for people with impaired hearing, but can be frustrating for those with impaired vision or mobility.)

The Venue

Where will it take place—in your church, in a church hall, or somewhere out of doors? Churches and the great outdoors often have interesting nooks and crannies that make excellent settings for prayer stations. Church halls tend to be boring rectangles, but at least they have flat floors, which can make the marking of a path easier. Of course, if you decide on a prayer fayre rather than a journey, there is no need to mark anything. Do you need to spring-clean the venue first?

The Timing

When will it happen? As suggested above, it may just be for a couple of hours—or it could be for a couple of weeks. Or it may begin with just one or two prayer stations, with others being added gradually, perhaps during Lent. Obviously space is likely to be a key factor, as would be the need to 'staff' the installation if there were security issues (for example valuable equipment) or safety issues (for example lighted candles). If you have room, you may be able to leave the prayer stations set up whilst other activities take place, which means that people who might not otherwise visit the prayer stations will be able to see what it is all about.

The Team

Who is going to do the work? Better a team than one person working alone. This is the kind of task where different creative minds spark one another off, and where different gifts complement each other. And a variety of input is likely to produce a variety of output—a wide range of prayer stations appealing to people with different personalities and different approaches to spirituality. You may choose to give each team member complete responsibility for one or more stations—or you may want to work on stations together. In particular you might ask one person to write or print the texts for all the stations (and laminate them?), to give a consistency of presentation. Remember too that the 'work' is not just the design and preparation, but also involves publicity, welcoming people, supervision and maintenance—and dismantling everything afterwards! A significant time commitment is needed—but the organizers do find it rewarding.

The Publicity

If your prayer journey or prayer fayre is open to all, it is worth advertising it as widely as you can. Consider:

- parish magazines, church newsletters, local papers and radio stations;
- church and community noticeboards;
- church and community web sites;
- deanery and diocesan networks, churches of other denominations, ecumenical groups, religious communities.

It is useful to produce plenty of small invitations for liberal distribution among friends and contacts. You might like to leave some invitations at the end of your prayer journey for participants to take for their friends. No matter how thorough your advertising and promotion, a personal recommendation still works best.

The Purpose, Values, and Theme

Can you be specific about what you want to achieve with this prayer journey, other than 'bringing people closer to God'? Clearly one cannot be too prescriptive here, as each individual is being given some freedom to react in their own way to the ideas presented. But are you hoping for, for example, a new commitment to service? A deeper appreciation of a Scripture passage? A new understanding of God's wonderful love? Will your stations reflect your values regarding Scripture, freedom, and the diversity of creation (to give just three examples)? What unifying theme will your journey have? The overall coherence of a prayer journey can be enhanced by the use of a 'house style' for the explanations and, for example, by using the same table coverings for each station, or having a tea-light on each, or a flower. You may want to write a general introduction on a flipchart at the beginning, welcoming people and introducing the journey (see Example A in Chapter 5).

You may even want to produce a mini-guide with a general introduction and an overview of the stations, perhaps with spaces for people to write down their insights and responses. And, if you have the means to do so, it can be very effective to project one or more PowerPoint loops, creating a continuously changing visual background to reinforce your theme—either using your own digital photos, or downloaded images from an internet image search facility.

The Resources

Is your Christian community putting funds or materials at your disposal? Will you have to contribute something yourselves? Will you encourage donations from the participants? You may be able to economize by borrowing or scavenging the things you need, but have an eye for quality. There is a lot to be said for a deliberately 'low-tech' approach, but perhaps the most important thing is to encourage everyone in the planning team to use their own particular creative gifts.

Marking the Trail

There are lots of options here:

- a floor covering with sticky tapes or painted lines;
- using chairs, tables or portable screens or display boards to constrain people to your chosen route round the building;
- giving people a brightly coloured ribbon, not necessarily on the floor, to follow;
- laying a trail of carpet tiles, arrows or cut-out foot prints.

Outdoor venues can be marked with stones, bricks, logs, bales of straw—or, in grass, by mowing strips to make paths.

Safety is always a consideration. Avoid trip hazards, electrical hazards, fire hazards—and check your public liability insurance!

Designing the Stations

Sue Wallace has gathered together lots of helpful ideas[19]—but you can be creative yourself. For example, supposing you wanted to create a 'sorry' station, you could start by listing some of the metaphors and images you associate with repentance and forgiveness— turning back, letting go, washing away, rubbing out, burning up, throwing away—and so on. Then consider how you could turn one of these into 'active prayer,' involving a symbolic object and a symbolic action. If you are exploring a particular Scripture, does the Bible passage itself suggest something that you could reproduce or model?

How can you engage people's various senses? Look around your home or place of work or local shops or market—what is there that you could press into service as the core activity for a prayer station? Look for balance and variety; if all your stations involve buttons, think again! Remember that some people are sensate and others more intuitive, and some are more comfortable with thinking while others prefer feeling.

Are your instructions clear? Do they restrict or encourage the imagination?

Are your instructions clear? Do they restrict or encourage the imagination? Do you need to test some of your activities on a willing 'guinea pig'? Consider the visual impact of your stations—will they all look the same? Think about height, size, and colour. Do you need to bring in a small table or a stool to put things on? Would an old curtain or a tablecloth make a good backdrop? Can you enhance the effect with pictures or photos or artefacts? For example, you could decorate a pray-for-your-family prayer station with children's paintings of families, or adorn a pray-for-the-world station with carvings from other continents.

Sound

Is the place you have chosen naturally quiet, or do sounds filter in from outside? Would some background music help to mask the ambient noise and the sounds made by the participants? What kind of music will set the tone, without distracting? Or would the sound of waves or a stream be better? If you are using more than one room, you may want to create different moods by playing different kinds of music in each. You might even be able to organize live music for some or all of the time.

For the St Paul's Cathedral labyrinth, each participant was given a portable CD player with sounds and instructions to listen to. You might want to do the same. You could borrow a few personal CD players, and ask people to bring their own. The average computer sold today has a drive that can write CDs, and the software needed to prepare a soundtrack is readily available. So you may well have the technical resources to produce CDs with the sounds you want. But be warned that the preparation of this kind of soundtrack takes a fair amount of skill and a surprising amount of time.

Lighting

You may want to lower the main lighting in the room, and illuminate the stations with spotlights, standard lamps or candles. Subdued lighting can create a sense of security which may be conducive to opening up to God in new ways, so if you are using an area with an abundance of natural light, you might consider some form of blackout. Cellars and basements offer special advantages here.

Traffic Jams

Consider how long it will take the average participant to work their way along the route. How many participants can the journey hold at one time? Will you start people at intervals of one minute, five minutes or more? Where will people wait at the beginning, and what might they do while they are waiting? You might provide some kind of craft activity, or simply something to colour (perhaps some Celtic designs); either of these could be done alone or as a group activity. Some people may wish to return to this activity after their journey.

It helps if at least some of your stations allow for the interactive presence of more than one person. Assure participants that it is all right to overtake — and to be overtaken! If you anticipate a lot of visitors in a short time, a prayer fayre may be more realistic than a prayer journey.

Maintenance

From time to time while the prayer journey is in use, somebody should check that the stations are all in good working order, replacing candles or pens, refilling jugs or doing whatever needs doing.

Follow Up

Some people will be deeply touched by the experience. It is good to have somebody on hand to offer a chat and/or prayer.

Feedback

A visitors' book or a graffiti sheet at the end of the journey will help the participants to learn from their journey, and will help you realize how effective your work has been. Or you might like to solicit some reactions by phoning or emailing a sample of the participants the next day. Be ready to build on what you learn!

5

Some We Made Earlier

Here are a few examples of prayer journeys to inspire you.

Each is reported in its own way. In some cases we reproduce only the text displayed at each station, and leave you to deduce the equipment used. In the last example we explain the equipment, and leave you to deduce the text. In all cases, we trust we have given you enough information to visualize something like the original prayer journey—and maybe to use it as a springboard for your own creative adventure. Some plans, photos, and more examples will be found on the Grove Books web site.

Example A: Elijah

This example was supplied by Patrick Angier, Curate at Holy Trinity, Stratford-upon-Avon and was first used in 2000 at Soulfire, the youth worship at All Saints Bedworth.

If this is the first time you have seen or walked a labyrinth then don't panic! There is only one route through, there are no dead ends or wrong turns so you cannot be lost. The route can be walked as slowly as you wish. Along the way you will be able to read Elijah's experience from 1 Kings printed out on cards on the floor so there is no need for you to take a Bible.

There will also be seven stations with activities and reflections to help you engage with the Scripture passage and with God. You need not do them all. Travel at whatever speed you are comfortable, fast or slow. Spend as much time as you need at each station; overtake others if you want to, but they may be deep in prayer so try not to disturb them. If you do have to wait at a station then use the time to be still and reflect on the journey so far.

The path will take you towards the middle of the labyrinth and then back out again and the exit is at the far end of chapel. The space beyond the labyrinth is for reflective prayer and listening to God. There is no hurry—you can spend as long as you wish there. When you have finished, walk around the outside of the labyrinth (rather than back through it) to the chapel entrance and return to the front lounge where there will be refreshments available.

a Entrance
Elijah had defeated the prophets of Baal on Mount Carmel; God had vindicated Elijah's faith. Jezebel's mercenary prophets were put to the sword and

the long drought, the curse on the land, is ended. This was a moment of triumph for Elijah and for the God of Israel. But we do not find Elijah celebrating, making the most of his new popularity amongst a fickle people. Instead we find him fleeing.

As we walk and pray our way around the labyrinth we will journey with Elijah from one mountaintop experience down across the desert until eventually reaching another mountain, Mount Horeb, where God speaks to him again.

b Mountaintop

Mountaintop experiences are great—those times when we experience God in new, deeper more exciting ways.

Think about a mountaintop experience for you. It could be a Christian conference, the realization of your call, a retreat or a specific answered prayer. Reflect on how you felt, how it encouraged you, how you think about it today. As you reflect on the experience choose and light a candle and add it to the display.

c Realization

With Jezebel's message came realization for Elijah—this was not the end, it was only the beginning. Jezebel would hire in a new batch of Baal prophets and a fickle people would turn away again from Yahweh. God's triumph on Mount Carmel would be soon be forgotten and Elijah's life and mission would be rapidly terminated.

Elijah's assessment of his situation, like many post-mountaintop comedowns, was over-pessimistic and did not truly reflect his position. Our assessment of our own situation can often be marred and confused.

Kneel by the side of the red tub, and look at your face reflected in the mirror in it. Stir the waters, to remind you of the concerns that surround you, the anxieties that persecute you, the voices of doubt that can pursue you.

See how your image, the image created by God, becomes marred and distorted. Now still yourself. Watch your image come back into focus. Be still, come into God's presence and allow the distractions to subside so you can see who you truly are.

d Fear

Elijah was beset by fears, and as he dwelt on them they began to overwhelm him. What is the fear which most overwhelms you? Write it in the sand.

Then take a handful of the sand, sprinkle it over the letters until they merge into the sand again and are lost. As you do so ask God to do the same to your fears and anxieties, not to bury them but to melt them away with his transforming presence.

e Water

Without water in the desert a traveller soon dies; it is the same for us in our spiritual lives. Elijah needed both food and water for his journey. Take a glass and fill it with some water and drink it. Ask God to refresh you.

f Bread

Elijah was brought bread and water to nourish him for his journey. Take a piece of bread. As you eat it ask God to nourish and resource you in the week ahead.

g Time

We live in a culture of instant gratification—fast food, instant communication, pre-packaged, throwaway, disposable. This secular value has infected much of our faith life as well. Scripture has a different timeframe. Women and men of faith spent not just days but often weeks and years waiting for God to answer prayers or fulfil his promises. Think of examples of waiting you can recall from Scripture.

Elijah travelled for forty days and forty nights. Very quietly read the prayer on the sheet (a version of St Patrick's breastplate) a line at a time. At the end of each line take one of the blue stones out of the bowl and place it beside you to represent the forty *days*. Repeat the process reading the prayer one line at a time and at the end of each line take one of the stones from beside you and place it back into the bowl to represent the forty *nights*. Reflect on this time of waiting. Why did God not meet with Elijah where he was? Why did he have to journey on?

h Despair

Elijah had reached the point of despair; he had exhausted his own strength. The memory of his mountaintop experience could not resource him further, so he calls out to God to let him die. Pick up one of the rucksacks and put it on; feel the weight dragging you down. By relying on our own strength we will become worn out and exhausted, unable to go on.

Look back towards the first labyrinth station and remember the mountaintop experience you lit a candle for. Look at your candle; does it burn brightly or is it a fading glory? Relying only on our past experiences will not provide resources for our ongoing journey. Feel the weight of the rucksack and the ache of the straps. When you feel ready to stop relying on yourself, take off the rucksack. Look back towards the mountaintop and when you are ready, move on.

i Exit

Elijah came to Mount Horeb and went into a cave and spent the night. The next day there was a mighty wind, then there was an earthquake, and after the earthquake a fire, but the Lord was not in these. Then came a still small voice. Find a space where you can relax and be still, and listen to that still small voice calling you.

Example B: Lord's Prayer

This example was supplied by Paul Breckell[20] and was first used by an alternative worship group at his Baptist church in Hemel Hempstead.

a Our Father, who art in heaven
Spend some time with the Father, using images of the Son.

b Hallowed be thy name
Read these poems, psalms, hymns and stories. Read them alone, or read them to one another.

c Thy kingdom come, thy will be done, on earth as it is in heaven
Take a look at the kingdom of God, now, on earth. Imagine. Imagine what it might be like, when God's will is done on earth, as in heaven. Imagine.

d Give us this day our daily bread
Count out thirty of the barley grains; the pile of grain represents the population of the world. Each grain represents 200 million people. Use the following ways of dividing the grain into two piles as a meditation on the theme 'give us this day our daily bread.'

- Take fifteen of the grains to make a new pile; this is the number of people who live on less than £1 per day. Put the grain back again.
- Take six grains to make a new pile; this is the number of people who do not have access to fresh drinking water. Put the grain back into one pile.
- Take five grains to make a new pile; this is the number of people who cannot even sign their own names (three of these grains represent women). Put the grain back into one pile.
- Take three grains to make a new pile; this is the number of people who are severely malnourished in the world today. Put the grain back into one pile.
- Take six grains to make a new pile; this represents the 1.2 billion people who spend 90% of the world's wealth (each of us here is one of them). Look at how many grains are left. Put the grain back into one pile.
- Take three of the grains to make a new pile; this represents the people who use 90% of the world's fresh water (each of us in this room is one of them). Look at how many grains are left.

Give us this day our daily bread. Amen.

e Forgive us our trespasses
Take a slate; use the chalk, and write or draw on it something to signify
things that you do wrong. Something specific or general. Wet the slate and
wipe it clean. Drop the slate into the water.
He will forgive our sins and purify us from all our wrongdoings. 1 John 1.9

f As we forgive those who trespass against us
Take a slate, use the chalk to write or draw on it something to signify things
that people have done to us, people we need to forgive. Something specific
or general. Wet the slate and wipe it clean. Drop the slate into the water.

Then Peter came to Jesus and asked, 'Lord, if my brother keeps on sinning
against me, how many times do I have to forgive him? Seven times?'
'No, not seven times,' answered Jesus 'but seventy times seven.' Matthew 18.21

g Lead us not into temptation, but deliver us from evil
Take a compass. The compass will always point north. Place it on the map,
and imagine the compass is pointing toward God, plotting your journey.
Now pick up one or more of the magnets. Place them on the map. Move
them toward to compass; see what happens to the needle.

The magnets are the things that interrupt your journey, distract you, lead
you in other directions. Can you name them? Can you identify them to yourself? Can you pray about them?

h For thine is the kingdom, the power and the glory, for ever and ever. Amen
Praise God. Thank God. Be still with God. When you feel ready, light a candle to signify his power and glory. Place the lit candle on one of the letters
that spells 'AMEN' in the centre of the labyrinth.

Example C: Your Kingdom Come

*Prepared by Sally Dakin and Paula Pocock for a day of prayer in the Archdeaconry
of Berkshire, November 2003.*

First choose either path A or path B:

Path A
Large collection of small plastic animals, birds, fish, and insects. Look at
them, identify with one, and think what you have in common with it!
Talk to God about these aspects of yourself, and know how much he
loves you.

Paper, pencils, paper shredder. Reflect on any 'litter' in your life that you are ready to get rid of. Write it down on a piece of paper, then feed the paper through the shredder, and receive God's forgiveness.

'Five senses' display—flowers, chocolates, essential oils, wind chimes, lambskin. Take time to enjoy what you 'sense' and give thanks to God.

Path B

Display of various nuts and fruits, some open. Choose one, and open it if you like. Reflect on your own openness to God and others—and on how your inside compares with your outside. Talk to God about these things, and know he loves you inside out.

Large bowl of water and towel. Identify any areas of your life where you would like to be washed clean. Put your hands into the water and receive God's forgiveness.

Branches in pot, small coloured cards, scissors, felt-tips, hole-puncher, thread. Cut a card into a leaf, flower or fruit shape, and write something you are thankful for, then hang it on the 'Thankyou Tree.'

Now go to the 'throne' in the centre...

'Throne' on red carpet, draped with velvet, fairy lights and lots of art/craft materials, especially shiny, sparkly things, and tools. Use the materials in any way you like to decorate the throne for the King of Kings. Offer your work and your worship to him, and pray that his kingdom will come in your life, your church and your community.

Now choose either path C or path D:

Path C

Twisted wires mounted in solid base, beads. For each friend or relative you would like to pray for, take a bead. As you thread it onto the 'Bead Tree' bring this person and his or her needs to God.

A5 card, wax crayons, paint, brushes and water. Take a crayon and a card, and write or draw a situation or place in the world you are concerned about. Brush over the card with watery paint, praying for God's justice and peace and healing.

'Crown' flags drawn with gold pens on sticky labels, stuck on toothpicks, inside a gold crown. The King is coming! How might you prepare to welcome him? Take a flag as you leave as a sign of your readiness.

Path D

Bag of Scrabble letters, alphabet stickers, stencils, felt-tips, A1 paper. Take a letter out of the bag and choose someone whose name begins with that letter. As you stencil or stick the person's initial on the paper, pray for him or her.

Map of the world (green on blue paper tablecloth), white felt doves, needles and thread, scissors. Sew a cross to mark a place which is special to you, or sew a dove in a place of pain. Hold the edge of the map and pray for God's Spirit of peace to fill his world.

Various clocks, watches, egg timers and clock face rubber stamp and ink pad. The King is coming! But we do not know when. How best can you use your time before he comes? As you leave, stamp your hand with the clock face and offer all your time to him.

Example D: Five Themes for Mission

Prepared by Matt Ward, Anglican Chaplain at the University of Coventry, for the Church Mission Society Conference in Coventry, November 2003.

A labyrinth design (no branches, but with separate entrance and exit) was marked on large tarpaulin. The overall shape was a Mercian cross. Simple materials and techniques were used to construct five stations based on the CMS priorities for mission where the name of Jesus is rarely heard.

a Mission in a Materialist World
Plastic boxes illustrating different aspects of the unjust sharing of the world's resources, for example nine batteries for developed world, one for the rest.

b Mission Amongst Those of Other Faiths
A large cross was made of strings. Participants were invited to weave a length of coloured wool through the strings while praying about somebody of another faith.

c Mission in the City
A gazebo frame was used to support a number of hanging cloths, creating a labyrinth within the labyrinth. All the cloths had images of tower blocks painted on, with words like despair, poverty. The last one has positive words such as love, help, and welcome, forming the shape of a cross.

d Mission on the Margins
A poster was displayed about an Indian community that makes palm crosses. Participants were invited to make crosses out of strips of paper, to write on prayers for marginalized people, and stick them on the board.

e Mission Among Women, Children and Young People

This station was designed to illustrate the concept of bringing light into people's lives. Looking through a peephole in the side of a large black dustbin, participants could barely see words of hope illuminated by an ultra-violet lamp. The top of the bin was covered with thick card on which was written the names of things which harm young people, such as AIDS. Participants were invited to pierce holes through the card, to let more light into the darkness.

Outside Options

We have already mentioned the possibility of setting your prayer journey in the open air. You could use a churchyard, the grounds of a school or a conference centre—perhaps even a local park, after negotiation with the appropriate authorities.[21] The advantage of having more space to play with is obvious. The disadvantages could be distractions from the surroundings, and the possibility of inclement weather ruining your stations and dampening the enthusiasm of your participants.

But why set up stations when there are things to see and do ready and waiting for you? The Touchstone Chaplaincy in Bradford[22] has produced a prayer walk leaflet, guiding people on a circular route through the city centre with eleven points for meditation and prayer.[23] Is this something you could do for the place where you live? Most of the activities in the Bradford leaflet are cerebral, but perhaps you could incorporate more physical things—touch a statue, feed the ducks, pick up some litter.

A number of people have experimented with the idea of a 'retreat on the streets,' taking the time to look at, reflect on, and pray for their neighbourhood,[24] but this is a more corporate activity, with time reporting back to the group at the end of each session.

Commuters might use the landmarks that they see each day on their journey as stimuli for reflection and prayer

Another suggestion[25] is that commuters might use the landmarks that they see each day on their journey as stimuli for reflection and prayer. In a suburban parish it would be possible to gather together a number of commuters who use the same route to agree a common list of landmarks and their significance, bearing in mind of course the different vistas offered by different seats on the train or bus.

6

By now you are probably full of enthusiasm and ready to set up a full-scale prayer journey for your Christian community!

If you choose (and publicize) an appropriate time and place, and find one or two others to work with, you will be almost certainly be able to design and set up something which people will come to and which God will use.

If this would be too much (for you or the church!), 'active prayer' can be introduced quite discreetly by creating occasional prayer stations on the edge of the worship space, perhaps at the back of the church or in a Lady Chapel in Lent or Holy Week. It seemed to happen quite spontaneously during the Iraq war, with the lighting of candles being a popular form of active prayer.

Active prayer can also be introduced within the service of worship itself and in fact those who plan all-age worship often do this instinctively. For example, in a Family Service with 'Building and being built' as its theme, the congregation were invited to collect a brick from the back of the church, put their name on it, and bring it up to the front, in order to build a wall together. At the end of the service, after showing some slides of the Western Wall in Jerusalem, people were invited to write a prayer on a piece of paper, fold it up small and poke it into a gap in the 'wall.' So those present both created and used the prayer station, in a way which allowed for both corporate and individual meanings.

Specific art or craft activities can be particularly helpful in encouraging active prayer in all-age worship. Whether the activity is an individual one (modelling yourself in playdough) or a corporate one (group paintings about 'war,' 'peace,' and so on) it can be followed by an 'offertory' of some kind, perhaps bringing the finished work up to the communion table.

And of course active prayer can be introduced into adult worship, though perhaps it is worth experimenting in an evening service, or in a special service like Good Friday, or on a parish weekend, before launching anything too unusual on the main Sunday morning service! There may also be opportunities to enrich the pastoral liturgies of baptism, marriage and funerals with symbolic objects and actions designed to meet the needs of a particular situation.

Those who are used to working with children and young people may have all sorts of skills and experience to bring to 'active prayer,' as may the children and young people themselves and those with a background in art or design. But as long as you are prepared to think 'out of the box' and to trust your creative instincts, anyone can design prayer stations. To illustrate this, a group with no prior experience of active prayer were divided into threes and each triad was given at random a card saying, 'Thank you,' 'Sorry' or 'Please,' and another card suggesting an object—seeds, feathers, water, candle, leaves, coins, oil, bread, grapes. They were asked to devise prayer activities using the combination they had been given, such as thanksgiving using seeds. All the triads came up with several useable ideas, thus providing a powerful antidote to the 'I'm not very creative' thinking which can keep our prayer life, both individual and corporate, stuck in a rut.

Once people get un-stuck, and active prayer begins to be an acceptable part of corporate worship, it is likely to flourish in the life of the church's small groups, as leaders begin to think creatively about how to encourage group members to grow in prayer. People may become less inhibited, both in prayer and in talking about their prayer life and spiritual experience, and the resulting openness may stimulate a new desire to learn and grow in prayer. It may also encourage a fresh approach to Scripture, especially where prayer stations and prayer journeys are inspired by particular passages, and people are invited to engage in a new, active way with God's word. We are not the first to discover that prayer can be truly active and spirituality can be truly multi-sensory:

> That which was from the beginning, which we have heard, which we have seen with our eyes, which we have looked at and our hands have touched—this we proclaim concerning the Word of life. (1 John 1.1)

Notes

Website addresses were current in June 2004 and can all be found under Online Resources on the Grove Books web site www.grovebooks.co.uk.

1   In February 2004 the Church Pastoral Aid Society (CPAS) launched a national initiative called *Firestarters* encouraging prayer for children, using the prayer fayre format. Resource material is available on the web, via www.cpas.org.uk.
2   See Paul Roberts, Grove booklet W 155 *Alternative Worship in the Church of England*.
3   WH Matthews, *Mazes and Labyrinths—their history and development* (London: Longmans, 1922; republished New York: Dover, 1970).
4   H Kern, *Through the Labyrinth, Designs and Meanings over 5000 years* (English edition, London–Munich–New York: Prestel, 2000).
5   Matthews p 54, illustration p 55; Kern, p 28, illustration p 88.
6   See the two books already mentioned, also P Conty, *The Genesis and Geometry of the Labyrinth: Architecture, Hidden Language, Myths and Rituals* (Rochester, Vermont: Inner Traditions, 2002).
7   See 'Way of the Cross' in the online Catholic Encyclopedia at www.newadvent.org.
8   Order from www.proost.co.uk.
9   www.yfc.co.uk/labyrinth/online.html
10 *Journey*—CDRom includes the 'virtual labyrinth' and a seven-week discipleship course—published by Proost/YFC.
11 See also Pete Greig and Dave Roberts, *Red Moon Rising* (Kingsway, 2004).
12 See for example Kern and Conty, and the websites www.labyrinthsociety.org and www.labyrinthos.net.
13 Jim Buchanan projected a labyrinth into a swimming pool, www.landartist.co.uk; Jill Geoffrion at www.jillkhg.com , and www.labyrinthcompany.com.
14 For example Jill Geoffrion, *Praying the Labyrinth: A Journal for Spiritual Exploration* (Cleveland: Pilgrim Press, 1999).
15 It may also raise the theological question: is God's will for us a single path, or does he let us use our free will in choosing between options which in his sight are equally good?
16 *Cataphatic*—affirming the immanence of God and his presence in the created order, as opposed to *apophatic*, reflecting on the transcendent mysteries of God.
17 A more robust Good Friday activity is hammering nails into a wooden cross.
18 Or even Orthodox prayer cords, often used with the Jesus Prayer. See Simon Barrington-Ward, *The Jesus Prayer* (Oxford: BRF, 1996).
19 Sue Wallace, *Multi-sensory prayer* and *Multi-sensory Church* (Bletchley: SU, 2000, 2002).
20 Paul was one of the planning team for *Worship Space*, an alternative worship group supported by Baptist churches in Hemel Hempstead. He is also the Finance Director of the Church Mission Society.
21 In Milton Keynes there is a permanent labyrinth marked in the grass by Willen Lake, which has been used as a prayer labyrinth, with the addition of stations, by Christians.
22 Established in 1989 as a Methodist presence in the city centre of Bradford—a church presence without a congregation serving not only Methodists but also the wider church in its work with communities across Bradford and West Yorkshire. See www.touchstone-bradford.org.uk/index.htm.
23 From an original idea by members of 'HOST alternative worship' and Bradford University Christian Union.
24 One resource for this is a booklet by Simon Bailey, *Stations—places for pilgrims to pray* (Cairns Publications, 1991).
25 From Rt Revd Colin Buchanan, Bishop of Woolwich. See also Andy Rider, Grove Spirituality booklet S 87 *Time, Space and God: Spiritual Lessons in London's West End*.